The Roll Call
of the
Blessed Ones

by

Janos Starker

Illustrations by

Jorge Sicre

DORRANCE PUBLISHING CO., INC.
PITTSBURGH, PENNSYLVANIA 15222

This printing was made possible by
Symphony Studios, Max Hobart, Director,
5 Pond Circle, Boston, MA 02130.

ISBN # 0-8059-4117-7
Printed in the United States of America

First Printing 1985
Second Printing

For information or to order additional books, please write:
Dorrance Publishing Co., Inc.
643 Smithfield Street
Pittsburgh, Pennsylvania 15222
U.S.A.

ROLL CALL OF THE BLESSED ONES

Prologue

Nature bestows talent on individuals, who, through a mixture of gifts, digital, artistic, and charismatic, manage to attain the adoration of the public, often way beyond logic. This adoration is measured in sold-out houses, media acclaim, money, and short-lived "historic significance." This brief historic significance is the result of lists, books, and encyclopediae prepared by those who have not been as fortunate as the blessed ones, and have themselves gained respect as arbiters of taste.

From the vantage point of two whose qualifications equal those of the blessed ones and transcends those of the arbiters, here is a list, however subjective, of some active in anno Domini 1985.

We offer this book to the cello and its practitioners

DEDICATION

This book is dedicated to those included and omitted, whose lives are spent in single-minded pursuit of music, maybe the highest of all human endeavors; a pursuit that enriches the lives of millions as a by-product. To poke fun at individuals, whose superb output presupposes self-security and a sense of humor, is the same as political satire. As Saul Steinberg once said, "Parody is not an attack; you cannot parody anything you can't love." The authors have no axe to grind but for the disturbing significance attached to utterances arriving regularly from the mouths of such dominant figures. May we see more humility and dignity displayed toward our art and less self-aggrandizement.

This book has been ten years in the making. Many of the "blessed ones" have since joined heavenly philharmonics, international pantheons, or just social security systems. We salute them with love, admiration and eternal gratitude.

THE COMPOSER

PIERRE BOULEZ

The only free and sensitive human
computer in captivity

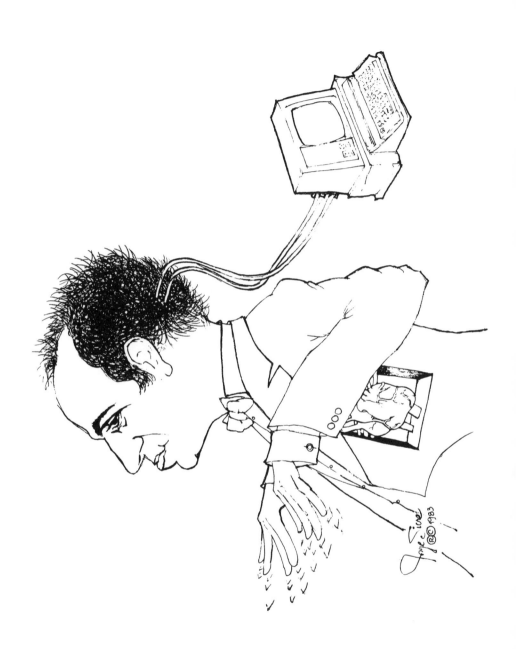

JOHN CAGE

The nemesis of piano technicians

AARON COPLAND

The first guest "en el salón" establishment

LUKAS FOSS

The most pragmatic mystic of them all

5

OLIVIER MESSIAEN

Birdom's greatest gift to mankind

6

KRZYSZTOF PENDERECKI

A Pole apart

GUNTHER SCHULLER

One who swims well in all streams

THE MAESTRO

DANIEL BARENBOIM

The little Napoleon who often omits days to stay
home for study without the public and fees

LEONARD BERNSTEIN

The greatest repository of all-around talent, 70%
used within and beyond music. Mr. Secretary in
the hoped-for U.S. Department of Culture

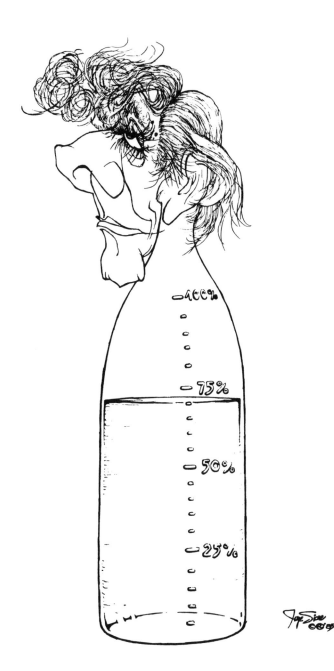

SARAH CALDWELL

Opera anyone?

ANTAL DORATI

Alias Joseph Haydn, Jr., who stopped getting mad
in time to be admired

RAFAEL FRÜHBECK DE BURGOS

The noble Don among the burgh-ers

CARLO MARIA GIULINI

The Virgin on the Island for Saints

HERBERT VON KARAJAN

History's first one-man musical conglomerate in
the mold of Howard Hughes and Frank Sinatra

ERICH LEINSDORF

One who scaled all the heights but missed many
of the sights

JAMES LEVINE

The Karajan of mid-Manhattan

LORIN MAAZEL

One of the few child prodigies alive who is even better and smarter today than at the age of 12

ZUBIN MEHTA

The unofficial president of Israel, soon to be
mayor of New York City, who could charm Arab
sheiks into buying tubas for his orchestra

SEIJI OZAWA

The boy wonder of the podium who passed through
adolescence courtesy of the great orchestras

ANDRÉ PREVIN

Hollywood's greatest gift to classical music

SIR GEORG SOLTI

The answer to universal energy shortage

KLAUS TENNSTEDT

The tenderest of Teutons

THE PIANIST

CLAUDIO ARRAU

One who played everything and became a star
in spite of himself

VAN CLIBURN

The slowest eyelid of the Southwest, or one who
spoke the least to the most

EMIL GILELS

The Russian variation of Enigma

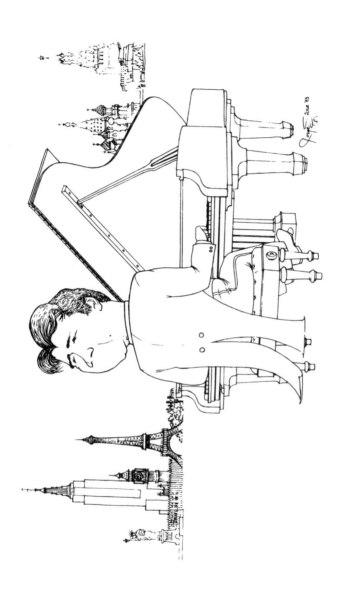

VLADIMIR HOROWITZ

History's greatest pianist on Sunday afternoons

ARTURO BENEDETTI MICHELANGELI

To play or not to play, that is the question

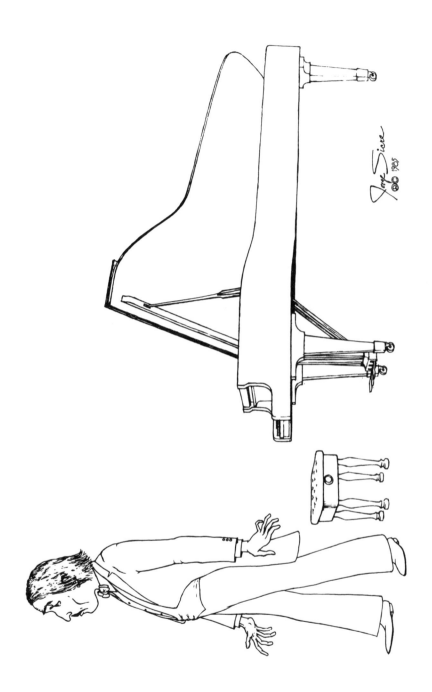

SVIATOSLAV RICHTER

The lonely survivor of the Romanovs. Had he been
born in New York he would have been Horowitz
and Rubinstein in one

RUDOLF SERKIN

The Santa Claus of the piano, bringing Christmas
wherever he goes

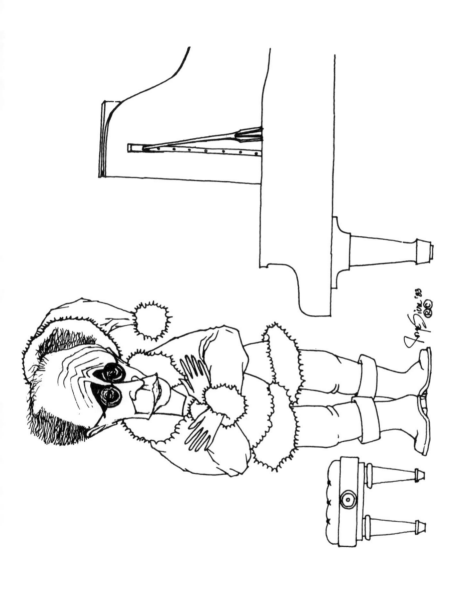

ANDRÉ WATTS

The dream answer to truly fair employment
practice

ALEXIS WEISSENBERG

Mirror, mirror on the wall, who is the most
beautiful pianist of them all?

THE VIOLINIST

GIDON KREMER

Kremer and Kremer versus Kremer

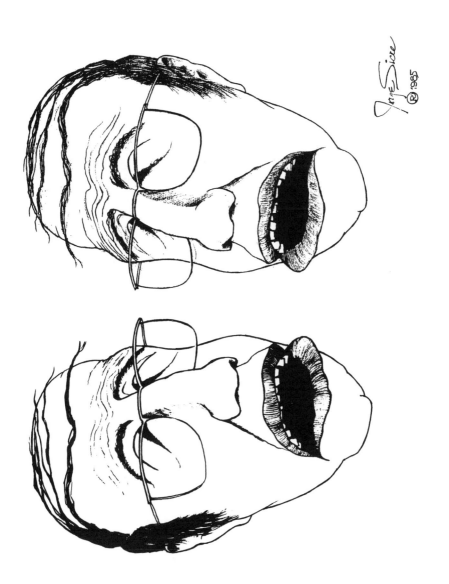

YEHUDI MENUHIN

The Pope Pius of the fiddle who bequeathed
himself at age 10

NATHAN MILSTEIN

One who long ago passed into history as a survivor
of an era; envied by today's hustlers, managers and
public relations experts alike

George Sicre '83

ITZHAK PERLMAN

Maybe the greatest of them all, who often forgot
that the dignity inherent in his work was more
important than a punch line to a story

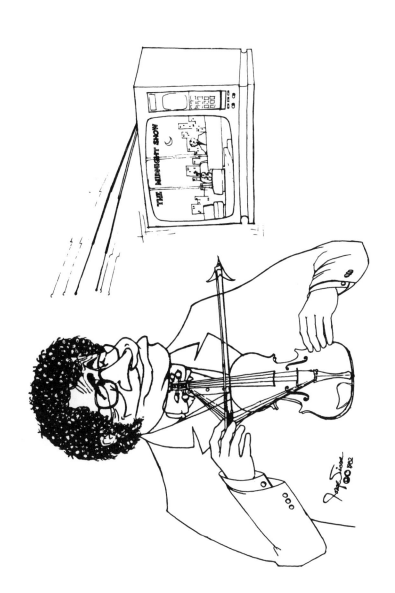

RUGGIERO RICCI

One who makes music at home and feeds
pyrotechnics to the plebs for Paga-(nini)

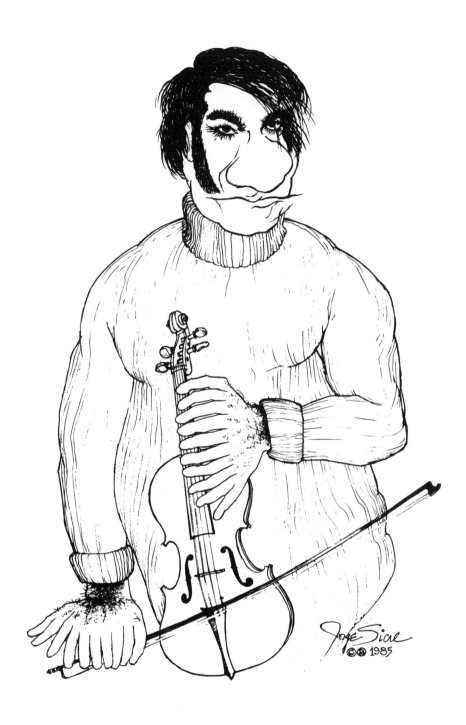

ALEXANDER SCHNEIDER

The first of all second fiddlers, whose greatest
glory lies in creating and catering to legends

ISAAC STERN

The Merchant of Cremona, fiddling his way from
roofs to D.C., into gray "eminence-ing" U.S. music

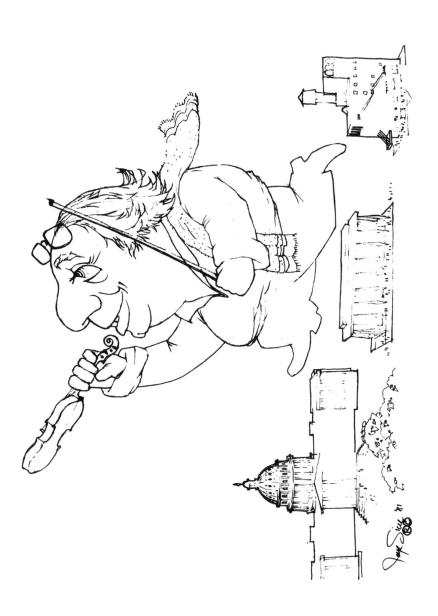

HENRYK SZERYNG

The impeccable linguist who still believes that fame
comes via titles and not vice versa

PINCHAS ZUCKERMAN

The "gang" member who used to think that the
world of music is but a tennis game where you win
or lose

THE CELLIST

PIERRE FOURNIER

One who dared to display humility and so
risked respect

ANDRÉ NAVARRA

The best fisherman among cellists

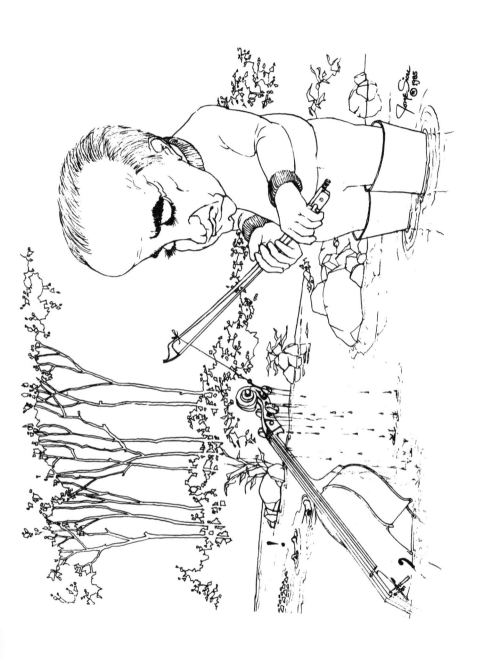

ZARA NELSOVA

The only cellist traveling with a balalaika

SIEGFRIED PALM

One who turned his troubles into an asset to produce ugly sounds on the altar of progressive music

MSTISLAV ROSTROPOVICH

The Bernstein of the cello: a one-man East-West
summit

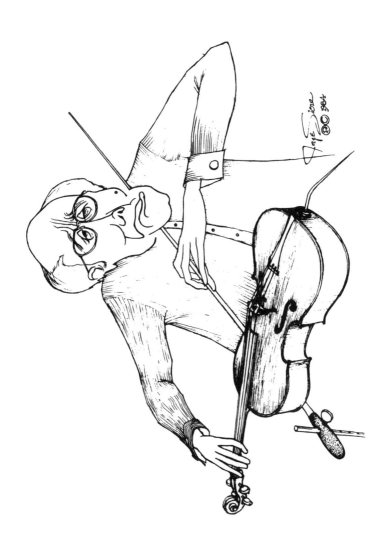

JANOS STARKER

One whose inner heat freezes the air around him
(Availability limited)

PAUL TORTELIER

Don Quixote reincarnate, fighting sheep and wind-
mills such as a former Nazi or a contemporary
composer

OTHERS

BEAUX ARTS TRIO

MENAHEM PRESSLER

No man's face has ever shown more love for music

ISIDORE COHEN

Me too

BERNARD GREENHOUSE

Bernie the sailor man

GARY KARR

Grand priest of the long-suffering bassists carrying
his message and instrumental hulk to all corners
of the globe

HARVEY PHILLIPS

Madison Avenue and Heifetz fused into one,
putting the tuba on the map

LUCIANO PAVAROTTI

The Rampal of the opera, having a ball with
his throat

JEAN-PIERRE RAMPAL

The Pavarotti of the flute, bon vivant, boy scout
and hero to an ever-increasing cult

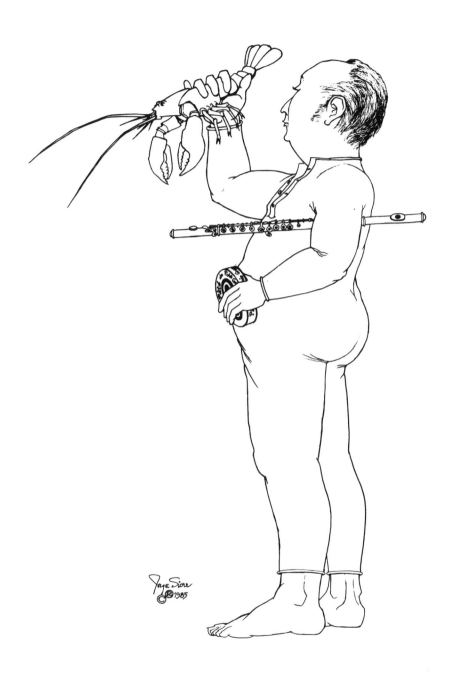

CODA

And then there are those who still work, suffer and
give immense joy to millions while satisfying
themselves.

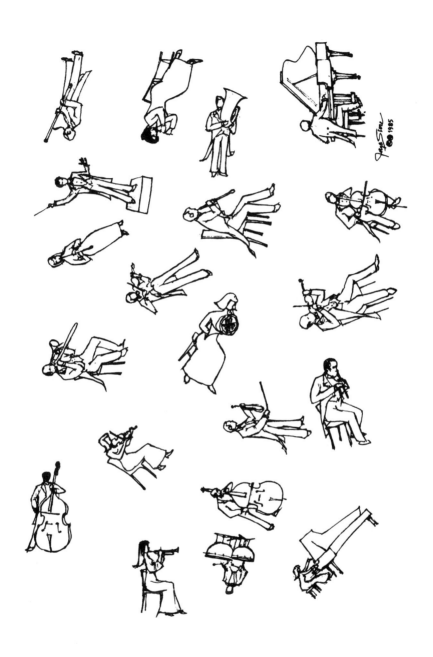

INDEX

23 A r r a u , C l a u d i o : pianist; has probably recorded and performed the widest repertory among all his contemporaries and successors; gloriously active in his eighties.

8 B a r e n b o i m , D a n i e l : pianist-conductor, music director of the Orchestre de Paris, guest conductor of all major orchestras, soloist, recitalist and ensemble player with the foremost instrumentalists and singers of the day.

9 B e r n s t e i n , L e o n a r d : pianist, composer, educator, writer, lecturer, conductor emeritus of the New York Philharmonic; he has done more for American musical life and music appreciation than anyone else alive or dead.

1 B o u l e z , P i e r r e : composer, conductor, former music director of the New York Philharmonic; director of Institut de Recherche et de Coordination Acoustique/Musique; one of the foremost exponents of 20th century music.

2 C a g e , J o h n : composer; his innovative ideas included altering or modifying the inside of the piano.

10 C a l d w e l l , S a r a h : conductor, founder and director of the Boston Opera company; her

dedication to promoting the opera culture of the U.S.A. is legendary.

24 C l i b u r n , V a n : pianist, first American to win the gold medal in the Tchaikovsky competition; his recording of the Tchaikovsky Concerto sold more copies than any other classical record.

48 C o h e n , I s i d o r e : violinist, Beaux Arts Trio; he joined the trio after the retirement of Daniel Guilet.

3 C o p l a n d , A a r o n : the doyen of American composers; the first 20th century American composer who gained the respect and acceptance of the musical establishment.

11 D o r a t i , A n t a l : pianist, cellist, conductor, composer, conductor emeritus of the Royal Philharmonic and the Stockholm Philharmonic, former director of the Russian Ballet, the Dallas Symphony Orchestra, the Minneapolis Symphony Orchestra, the Detroit Symphony Orchestra and the National Symphony Orchestra; his recordings include all the Haydn symphonies and most of the Haydn operas; his temper in his youth caused him union troubles.

4 F o s s , L u k a s : pianist, conductor, composer; presently music director of the Milwaukee Symphony Orchestra and the Brooklyn

Philharmonic; globe trotting performer whose works encompass the styles of the entire 20th century with stunning individuality.

41 F o u r n i e r , P i e r r e : cellist; one of the all time greats whose modesty and honesty placed music ahead of fame.

12 F r ü h b e c k d e B u r g o s , R a f a e l : conductor, former music director of Madrid's Orquesta Nacional. Frequent guest of all major orchestras of the world; his even-tempered elegant interpretations are much admired.

25 G i l e l s , E m i l : pianist, great virtuoso, among the first Russians to appear in the West; his reluctance to speak is legendary and his life is an unopened book.

13 G i u l i n i , C a r l o M a r i a : conductor, former music director of the Los Angeles Philharmonic, constant guest to major orchestras and opera houses of the world; admired for his honesty, sincerity and total dedication to his art.

48 G r e e n h o u s e , B e r n a r d : cellist extraordinaire, founding member of the Beaux Arts Trio; his major hobby is sailing.

26 H o r o w i t z , V l a d i m i r : pianist sans pareil, who, since a hiatus of years, restricts his public appearances to Sunday afternoons.

14 K a r a j a n , H e r b e r t v o n : conductor, music director of the Berlin Philharmonic, Vienna Philharmonic, Orchestre de Paris, Philharmonia, etc.: his recordings encompass the entire literature.

49 K a r r , G a r y : bass virtuoso; his international performing and pedagogic activities brought recognition not only to his great artistry but to the instrument as well.

32 K r e m e r , G i d o n : violinist, outstanding virtuoso; his demeanor on and off the stage often worries his admirers.

15 L e i n s d o r f , E r i c h : conductor, music director of the Rochester Philharmonic, the Cleveland Orchestra and the Boston Symphony, guest of all great orchestras and opera houses; his astonishing knowledge even as a youth stunned such greats as Toscanini; probably the least celebrated of the truly great conductors.

16 L e v i n e , J a m e s : pianist and conductor, music director of the Metropolitan Opera and Chicago's Ravinia Festival; he performs and records as a pianist with outstanding instrumentalists and singers.

17 M a a z e l , L o r i n : violinist, pianist, composer, conductor, film maker, music director of the RIAS, the Berlin Opera, the Vienna Opera

and the Cleveland Orchestra; his rare brilliance was first manifested in public as a child prodigy conducting the NBC Symphony.

18 M e h t a , Z u b i n : bass player, conductor, presently music director of the New York Philharmonic and the Israel Philharmonic, former music director of the Los Angeles Philharmonic and the Montreal Symphony Orchestra; a favorite of all major orchestras, whose ability to communicate with those responsible for running musical life is exemplary.

33 M e n u h i n , Y e h u d i : legendary violinist, violist, conductor, friend of heads of state, diplomat and loved by all; the most famous child prodigy of the century.

5 M e s s i a e n , O l i v i e r : organist, composer; one of the greats of 20th century music, whose works are imbued with a great deal of mysticism and sounds collected from a variety of our feathered friends.

27 M i c h e l a n g e l i , A r t u r o B e n e d e t t i : pianist, extraordinary performer whose frequent cancellations of concerts baffle his huge following.

34 M i l s t e i n , N a t h a n : violinist, the dean of the active virtuosi astonishing the world by his undiminished powers past 80.

42 N a v a r r a , A n d r é : cellist, teacher; performed all over the world and raised countless
cellists in France, Germany and Austria; major
hobby is fishing.

43 N e l s o v a , Z a r a : cellist, superb artist, the
greatest lady of the cello; credited with over-
coming the reluctance of airlines to permit
cellos on board by calling hers a balalaika.

19 O z a w a , S e i j i : conductor, presently music director of the Boston Symphony Orchestra, prior music director of Ravinia Festival,
the Toronto Symphony Orchestra, the San
Francisco Orchestra, guest conductor of all
major orchestras of the world.

44 P a l m , S i e g f r i e d : cellist, administrator
(director of the Berlin Opera); the most important figure in inducing contemporary composers to discover the cello; has first-performed
an immense number of works written for him
in all the prestigious musical centers of the
world.

51 P a v a r o t t i , L u c i a n o : grand tenor of
the world whose glorious voice set the world
on fire.

6 P e n d e r e c k i , K r z y s z t o f : composer,
one of the leaders of contemporary music;
known for his half and quarter tone clusters.

35 P e r l m a n , I t z h a k : violinist, superb virtuoso, frequent guest on national TV shows.

50 P h i l l i p s , H a r v e y : tuba virtuoso; his limitless ideas and energy produce mass tuba performances and tuba-fests in the major cities of the world.

48 P r e s s l e r , M e n a h e m : pianist and founder of the Beaux Arts Trio; his visible joy in performing the masters delights audiences everywhere.

20 P r e v i n , A n d r é : pianist, conductor, presently the music director of the Los Angeles Philharmonic, former director of the London Symphony and the Pittsburgh Symphony; his ability to transcend the tag of popular musician to arrive at the top of the classical musical scene astonished his peers.

52 R a m p a l , J e a n - P i e r r e : flutist; as Segovia brought the classical guitar into the mainstream of the world's musical life, so did Rampal for the flute.

36 R i c c i , R u g g i e r o : violinist; pegged as a Paganini specialist, his superb playing is restricted to a few concerts and friends.

28 R i c h t e r , S v i a t o s l a v : pianist; his eccentric, almost mystic, behavior has not diminished his superlative recreative artistry.

45 R o s t r o p o v i c h , M s t i s l a v : cellist, pianist, composer, conductor, music director of the National Symphony Orchestra; he performs all over the world and assists fellow Russians, politicians, business leaders and artists to improve human contacts.

37 S c h n e i d e r , A l e x a n d e r : conductor, violinist, for many years the superb second violinist of the Budapest String Quartet; his efforts in organizing the Prades and Puerto Rico Casals festivals earned him the gratitude of all musicians and music lovers.

7 S c h u l l e r , G u n t h e r : French horn player, conductor, composer; a towering figure in the world of music who successfully integrated jazz and classical idioms and called it the "third stream."

29 S e r k i n , R u d o l f : pianist, legendary for his superior artistry and the visible joy in his performances.

54 S i c r e , J o r g e : cellist, artist, Cuban-born member of a painter-sculptor family of several generations. Member of the Cleveland Orchestra.

21 S o l t i , S i r G e o r g : pianist, conductor, director of the Chicago Symphony since 1969, former music director of the Frankfurt, Munich, and Covent Garden operas and the

Orchestre de Paris; his boundless energy and drive astonish players and audiences alike.

46, 54 S t a r k e r , J a n o s : cellist, teacher; frequently described as cold and deadpan in his demeanor.

38 S t e r n , I s a a c : violinist; as chairman of Carnegie Hall he is advisor, member, chairman of national and international cultural organizations and has done more for the promotion of string playing and teaching than anyone else; his superb artistry was applied in the violin solo in the film "Fiddler on the Roof."

39 S z e r y n g , H e n r y k : violinist; his extraordinary playing has been rewarded with many national and international honors; he speaks fluently eight or nine languages and enough to converse in six others.

22 T e n n s t e d t , K l a u s : conductor, former music director of the North German Radio Symphony of Hamburg and since 1983 music director of the London Philharmonic and a favored guest of the leading orchestras of the world; he is admired for his lyric interpretation of the masters.

47 T o r t e l i e r , P a u l : cellist, composer; his performances of Strauss' tone poem are legendary; his wartime resistance and his active dislike of contemporary composers form part of

his significant contribution to the musical life
of Europe and elsewhere.

30 W a t t s , A n d r é : pianist; his stunning vir-
tuosity and artistry placed him among the
greats as a youth; he is the son of an American
father and a Hungarian mother.

31 W e i s s e n b e r g , A l e x i s : pianist; an
extraordinary performer who is also admired
for his impeccable attire.

40 Z u c k e r m a n , P i n c h a s : violinist, violist, conductor, music director of the Saint Paul
Chamber Orchestra, stunning virtuoso and
dedicated tennis player.